Explaining
The Grace
of God

Charles R. Strohmer

This Book Belongs to
Tim
Couchman

Sovereign World

Bible quotations, unless otherwise indicated,
are taken from the NIV The Holy Bible, New International Version.
© Copyright 1973, 1978, 1984 International Bible Society.
Published by Hodder & Stoughton.

KJV King James Bible.
Crown copyright.

ISBN: 1 85240 117 6

Also by Charles Strohmer:

What Your Horoscope Doesn't Tell You

Wise as a Serpent, Harmless as a Dove:
Communicating and Evangelizing in the New Age World

SOVEREIGN WORLD LIMITED
P.O. Box 777, Tonbridge, Kent TN11 9XT, England.

Contents

Preface and Acknowledgements   5

1   Grace in Genesis   7
    A working-definition; God coming down; the
    moving to well-being

2   Saving Grace   13
    Eternal well-being; spiritual and moral deliverance

3   Post-conversion Grace   19
    Righteousness; humility and pride; would-be
    disciples

4   Our Responsibility to Grace   27
    Obedience and disobedience; human weakness;
    indecision; grace swapping

5   Person-to-Person Grace Giving   35
    In the Old Testament; characteristics of today;
    approachableness

6   Spiritual Grace Giving   43
    God's gifts to the Church; their nature (what
    controversy?); the stewardship question; divine
    pliability

7   New Realities   53
    Inner and outer transformations; Christ's life of
    grace; the eclipse of hope; the return of a divine
    outlook

Preface and Acknowledgements

Many years ago, when I was a young Christian, I braved an agonizing period of pastoral counselling. I had been unexpectedly and dramatically "saved" after being deeply involved in occultism and New Ageism. Yet I had not been prepared by anyone for the implications of the radical change that occurs when one becomes a Christian, or how to live the Christian life. Pastoral counselling helped me find my Christian legs.

The dominant theme of the counselling was God's clear, strong call to me to "learn about grace". This sent me on a search not to amass intellectual knowledge on the subject, but to discover how to walk in grace and to have its transforming power in my life day after day. The call was so strong that the theme began to grow on me, and the result was that I spent several years studying the subject in the Bible, observing it in my life and in the lives of others, and doing a bit of teaching and writing about God's grace.

The greatest change in my understanding has been that what I once thought about God's grace now pales by comparison to what I know. And the biggest transformation in my life has been to enter the spiritual rest that such knowledge brings. This, I think, may be the foremost contribution of this booklet in the long run. It ought to be especially beneficial to those who, like myself, have struggled with Christianity more than it is popular to admit.

By some standards, I have had a rough Christian history. At times it has been very bewildering, difficult and depressing, and not only because of my own sins, failings and unwise choices. There are Christians who would say that what I have been through, not to mention my lack of "higher education", disqualifies me. To them I say that I know only too well I'm not good enough, not ready, not qualified to speak for and labour with God. But if God were limited to our qualifications or credentials, He would not call anyone. Here, then, is spiritual rest. When He calls, nothing can thwart the purpose of divine grace. Thus, neither an unworthy life nor a lack of credentials has prevented this little book from reaching you.

During the early days of study, prayer, observation and writing, I felt completely out of my depth with this subject. In particular, I want to thank Jeff, Charlotte and Ann for their prayers, suggestions and encouragement. Many thanks to you, too, Linda, for many stimulating conversations that helped me to be more gracious concerning some sensitive issues. And I am grateful to Chris Mungeam of Sovereign World Publishers for his willingness to take a risk with an "unknown", so that this message could travel beyond Jerusalem, Judea and Samaria to the ends of the earth.

Clearly, however, this booklet would be greatly lacking were it not for the gracious help of Rev. John Peck, theologian, philosopher and Baptist minister in Suffolk, England. Rev. Peck spent many hours pouring over this material in its larger format (as yet unpublished), out of which this booklet has been distilled. His theological and practical critique was like having a wonderful counsellor alongside me as I wrote.

Thank you, John, for covering my deficiencies, for time-consuming consultations and correspondence on issues that I would otherwise have missed, for giving me confidence, for helping me to clarify my thoughts, for making this worth publishing and in the process, for modelling to me how to live, think, walk and act more consistently out of a worldview whose twin points of focus are a manger and a cross, which brought us all the grace of God.

Nevertheless, I take responsibility for any errors or misrepresentations.

Finally, because this is a booklet and not a full-sized book, it may seem to ignore some aspects of doctrine and areas of dispute. That is because with a booklet one has only so much space. An editorial decision has been made to keep this material centred on a Life and how that Life influences and transforms our "lower case" lives. This Life has to be received and then lived out. Once we get up-and-running and begin to mature in this Life, there will be time for fine-tuning matters of doctrine and settling disputes. What I have tried to do here is to indicate how the grace of God gets us up-and-running in Life, and then to explain the basic ideas about how to live this Life in full bloom. Most other matters lie beyond the scope of this work. Besides, people in the full bloom of health, as someone has said, are not so interested in doctrine and disputes. They're too busy living.

1

Grace in
Genesis

It is through God's grace that Eternity lays hold of us and a relationship with God becomes possible that otherwise would not exist. And, yet, trying to describe this can be tough going. Indeed, God's grace is the subject of intellectual challenge and, at times, of controversy. It seems easier to describe other Christian realities like forgiveness, repentance or prayer.

There is no doubt that grace is a gift of God, and that it is at the very heart of the Good News, the Gospel. And grace is surprising too. It fills one with wonder and a gratifying, lasting sense of peace. This often happens unexpectedly, as it did with me seventeen years ago. I certainly was not looking for it. Does one look for the unknown? Yet just as certainly, and paradoxically, **when** surprised by grace, I knew without a doubt that it was what I had been looking for, that it was the one thing I had really needed all along.

Suddenly, unexpectedly, there it was: God's grace. It brought me into a relationship with God that otherwise would not have been possible. How does one describe this? An entirely new and previously unknown reality had tenderly burst in on me. I felt radically changed. I felt as if I had life for the first time. What had been "life", immediately became an old, used up thing. It looked rather silly compared to the new – shall I say "real" – life I had suddenly been given by God's grace. Somehow the old and the dying had been exchanged for the new and the undying. I do not mean this figuratively but literally. It really happened.

And it carried with it a sense of being rescued, for which I was deeply thankful. At the same time, other characteristics of grace clarified themselves in my mind. I knew I had no right to it, that I had not earned it, and that there was nothing of my own that had anything to do with it. I was twenty-six years old, and the mercy, mystery and power of it have grown on me ever since.

"Thanks be to God," wrote the apostle Paul, *"for his indescribable gift!"* (2 Corinthians 9:15). Paul, too, recognized the difficulty of describing that which makes the sinner a saint, the enemy of God His friend, the lost found, and the dead alive. Even today such a gift sounds strange to many people. Here in this booklet I would like us to try to remove some of the strangeness and unfamiliarity by looking at the subject of grace, not so much theologically, as practically.

The Christian life is an entire life of grace. Here, then, we are going to approach the subject as a formative principle and transformative dynamic for daily Christian living and activity. We are going to look at grace as the loving provision of God that shows us how to conduct ourselves both in the Church, and in the world at large. To do this, we will seek to identify the presence and purpose of grace within many experiences common to Christians, however much we may think that these experiences are bereft of grace.

This will take us into areas such as humility and discipleship, weakness and obedience, person-to-person grace giving, spiritual gifts, righteousness, and how we resist, or frustrate, God's grace. Look for a few surprises too! This is a practical exposition. Hopefully, it will be fresh and appealing. For some readers, it will be life-changing, as it was for me.

Grace in Genesis

To begin with, we need to do a little time-travelling back to the days of Noah and Lot. In Genesis, that book of beginnings, we will find a valuable working-definition for grace. Now things may seem a bit foreign in the distant past, but there we will find a good biblical foundation by which to make a start.

Noah and his family lived very early in human history. It was a time, the Bible says, when people began to increase on the earth (Genesis 6:1). During this period, and for reasons not entirely clear, human "wickedness" also increased greatly: *"Every inclination of the thoughts of* [everyone's] *heart was only evil all the time,"* (Genesis 6:5). As a result, the world became *"corrupt"* and *"full of violence,"* (Genesis 6:11). Left unchecked, it was not safe for anyone, and God stepped in to end it. Everyone was destroyed by a catastrophic flood that *"increased greatly on the earth* [until] *all the high mountains* [were] *covered... to a depth of more than twenty feet* [and] *every living thing that moved on the earth perished,"* (Genesis 7:18-21). (A number of ancient civilisations had accounts of a serious flood. These accounts have been discovered among the cuneiform documents excavated in the Near East; among them, Sumerian, Babylonian and Assyrian.)

This was not a decision God reached lightly. He says, *"As surely as I live... I take no pleasure in the death of the wicked, but rather that they may turn from their ways and live,"* (Ezekiel 33:11). It grieved God. It filled His heart with pain (Genesis 6:6). But not everyone died. At God's command, Noah and his family (eight persons) built a large wooden ship, the Ark, in which they gathered many animals and rode out the flood. Their lives were spared. Of this, the Bible says that *"Noah found **grace** in the eyes of the Lord,"* (Genesis 6:8). We will see the meaning of this statement and our working-definition shortly.

Similar but smaller in scale is the story of Lot. Centuries after the floodwaters had dissipated, and with the population rapidly increasing again, a certain cluster of cities had become extremely "sinful" (Genesis 18:20). The two cities most infamous for their brazen sin were Sodom and Gomorrah. Three others were Admah, Zeboiim and Bela or Zoar. These five made up the *"cities of the plain"* (Genesis 19:29), located near what is now the Dead Sea. The area was attractive from a material viewpoint, and it was here in a house in Sodom that Lot chose to live (Genesis 19:1-3).

Again, due to heightened sinful conditions, it was not safe for anyone (Genesis 19:4-10). God stepped in to end it, and once more His hesitancy and concern was evident (Genesis 18:16-33). This time, however, the judgement came not by water but by fire. God *"rained down burning sulphur on Sodom and Gomorrah – from the Lord out of the heavens. Thus he overthrew those cities and the entire plain, including all those living in the cities... [And] dense smoke rising from the land, like smoke from a furnace,"* (Genesis 19:24-25, 28). (Archaeological excavations show that a catastrophe at this time emptied the area of settlements for about 600 years.)

But not all the inhabitants perished. God sent two angels to save Lot and his family. Of this, the Bible says that Lot *"found grace"* in the sight of the Lord (Genesis 19:19). Whatever else was going through their minds, both Noah and Lot realised and acknowledged they had been spared by **grace**.[1] The grace for Noah was the Ark to ride out the storm, and the grace to Lot was an angelic visitation enabling escape from the fire (Genesis 6:13-7:7; 19:1-22). At this point we can say at least two things. One, that grace is God's loving provision; and, two, that it has something to do with being rescued. This brings us almost to our working-definition. To fully appreciate what that is, it is helpful to reflect first on the Old Testament idea of God "coming down".

God "Coming Down"

The Old Testament illustrates many instances of God "coming down" into human history to have a look around, so to speak, before He takes subsequent action. One time God came down to bring judgement during the building of the tower of Babel (Genesis 11:5–8):

> *"But the Lord **came down** to see the city and the tower that the men were building. The Lord said, 'If as one people speaking the same language they have begun to do this, then nothing they plan to do will be impossible for them. Come, let us go down and confuse their language so they will not be able to understand each other.' So the Lord scattered them from there over all the earth, and they stopped building the city."*

Another time, God "came down" upon Mount Sinai to bring the ten Commandments, or Law, to Moses, as recorded in Exodus 19:10-11:

*"And the Lord said to Moses, 'Go to the people and consecrate them today and tomorrow. Make them wash their clothes and be ready by the third day, because on that day the Lord will **come down** on Mount Sinai in the sight of all the people'."*

Another incident reveals God coming down to wage war (Isaiah 31:4):

*"The Lord Almighty will **come down** to do battle on Mount Zion and on its heights."*

The central theme of these passages (and others, too) is that God is active in human history. Now people may think God does not exist and that the universe, including ourselves, functions by blind chance or mere natural laws day after day. Others may think that God exists but that He is a kind of absentee landlord, a Being who created the universe, wound it up like a big clock, and then left it on its own to run (down). People may think these things, but such views have been given to us by our cultures. The Bible tells a different story. God is personally engaged in the activities of the universe, ourselves included, in giving law, executing judgement and waging war.

This idea of God personally coming down to us is fundamental to most uses of the Old Testament word for "grace", including those in the Genesis passages above. This is understood from its root word, which carries the idea of "bending" or "stooping" as a King might do to grant some favour to a subject. Thus the word also carries the idea of "favour" in the sense of **well-being**. And if we sum up these ideas we arrive at our working-definition, which is certainly not about God coming down to wage war, legislate or condemn. Far from it! Grace, then, is "God coming down **to move people to places of well-being**."

This initial revelation of grace in Genesis is foundational for the topic throughout the Bible. And it will be our working-definition throughout this booklet, as we try to discover the daily activity of grace in our lives.

[1]Most modern English translations of the Bible render the Hebrew word *chên* as "favour" rather than "grace", both in the Genesis passages and throughout the Old Testament. The King James Version usually renders *chên* as "grace" which is more to the point here. Therefore, though I am using the New International Version translation, which usually renders *chên* as "favour" I am taking the hint from the more literal King James Version and rendering *chên* as "grace" wherever "favour" appears in the New International Version. As a kind of universal human concept, "favour" may be thought of as being in some way earned through merit or behaviour. Yet the favour of God that is "grace" is different than all such human manifestations of favour, for the grace of God is utterly beyond the resources and power of man to earn, deserve or purchase.

2

Saving Grace

Having set forth the working-definition that grace is God coming down to move people to places of well-being, we may now turn to the beginning of the Christian life.

It is a common misunderstanding that the Christian life begins with physical birth, or by attending church, or by being born into a Christian family. As a result, the truly Christian life may be the most misunderstood kind of life. For instance, in America where I live, foreigners at times travel to our shores thinking they are coming to a Christian nation. Yet this myth is quickly exploded upon their arrival. Being born in America does not make one a Christian, any more than being born at MacDonalds makes one a hamburger! The Christian life has also been tragically mistaken as the producer of horrors like the Inquisition, the Crusades or the Nazi Holocaust. Others may think that the Christian life is the rituals and religious paraphernalia of Christianity, or its Church buildings, ecclesiastical structures or denominations.

The Christian life, however, has a distinct beginning, and that beginning is a gift. It is the gift of Life. Now this gift is from God and it is called His **grace**. God's gift of a new, an exchanged life is the central miracle of grace. It is the result of the Incarnation. God came down to be born as a man in Jesus Christ. And when He did, the most important event in human history happened, when Jesus Christ died on Calvary's Cross. Grace became available right here in this life, to give people God's life so that they could be moved to a place of **eternal** well-being.

When this gift is received, it is the start of the Christian life. Now, humanly speaking, it takes a certain kind of person to receive it. It takes someone who sees the point of the gift. And to see the point, one will have perceived something else prior to that. He will have understood his true human condition: that he is a sinner.

This is not to suggest that everyone practises evil continually. But neither is that to say we are basically good people who occasionally do bad. Rather, we are bad people who occasionally do good. God takes it for granted that we are bad. Until one feels this to be true about himself, he will see no point in the saving grace of Calvary.

The Problem of Slavery to Sin

Sin is an alien concept in a modern world that relies for its analyses of human nature upon psychoanalysis, self-improvement, self-esteem, human potential, New Age thinking and other self-help psychologies and philosophies. These pop-isms rob the modern world of any rhyme or reason for thinking about sin. The contention is that people are basically good; let's try to make them even better. Is it any wonder, then, that many people today place the reality of sin alongside that of UFOs? Incredible, but not to a few misguided souls.

But the person who feels his true human condition knows differently. He also knows something else: that there is not even the slightest possibility of remedial self-help from what the Bible calls sin. It is a disheartening situation, really. He feels the strength of sin within and wishes that he could be "saved" from it. But at the same time he recognizes himself as utterly powerless to change the situation.

The Bible paints no pretty picture of sin. It teaches that we are slaves to it. But what is sin? Short-listed, the *"acts of the sinful nature are obvious: sexual immorality, impurity and debauchery; idolatry and witchcraft; hatred, discord, jealousy, fits of rage, selfish ambition, dissensions, factions and envy; drunkenness, orgies and the like,"* (Galatians 5:19-21). This is an ugly but true picture, and we are slaves to it. The horridness of slavery may be something quite unimaginable to many readers here. Yet people who live under dictatorships or who have come out of totalitarian regimes will know it only too well.

The writers of the New Testament were familiar with slavery, and it gave them an accurate, alarming way to depict the human condition and the start of the Christian life. In a world under the influence of Roman law at the time of Christ, slaves were usually owned by people and so were without rights. They were just another piece of property to be used and disposed of as their owners saw fit. There were also Greek, Jewish and other kinds of slaves throughout the Mediterranean region. Some Christians, too, held slaves; and if so, the owners were commanded in the New Testament to govern with good will and affection, and Christian slaves were commanded to please God by their service (Ephesians 6:9; Philemon 8-14; Ephesians 6:5-8). Thus everyone in those days saw the conditions of slavery, which in most cases was utterly horrific.

This being so, Jesus easily made a point to His listeners about the human condition when He said, *"I tell you the truth, everyone who sins is a slave to sin,"* (John 8:34). Likewise, the apostle Paul was immediately understood by his Christian audience in Rome when he wrote that they had been *"slaves to sin"* and that slavery to sin *"leads to death,"* (Romans 6:16). In that world, everyone clearly knew that slavery ended with death. And Jesus and Paul heightened the human predicament by analogy to slavery. People are slaves to **sin** and so doomed to death. The ancient world would have understood. It may not have believed, but that is an entirely different matter. It would have understood.

The Solution is Redemption

Yet the ancient world would also have had something else come to mind, and it made the analogy even more apt. People would have regarded the situation as crying out for manumission. For, besides death, the preferable deliverance from slavery was release through payment of a price. This meant the buying or ransoming of the slave, which was called "redemption". Apart from redemption, slavery continued until death. This was a cold fact of life for slaves, and the people listening to Jesus or Paul would wonder if there were any kind of redemption from slavery to sin.

Yes, says the New Testament, redemption from sin is possible. There was a general practice in the ancient world that a slave could be bought and set free – redeemed – by being dedicated to the service of a god. A ransom would be put into the temple treasury and the slave would go through the formality of being sold to Zeus, Ares, Artemis or any god within the constellation of pagan polytheism. Through this process, the slave gained his freedom: a new life. The chief characteristic of the process was the payment of the ransom price and "redemption" was the name of the process.

When speaking of Jesus Christ and God's saving grace, the New Testament says, *"In him* [Jesus Christ] *we have **redemption** through his blood, the forgiveness of sins, in accordance with the riches of God's grace,"* (Ephesians 1:7; also see: Colossians 1:13-14). Here a distinctly biblical meaning is placed on the idea and practice of redemption and its price. The apostle Peter affirms the price, saying, *"For you* [Christians] *know that it was not with perishable things such as silver or gold that you were redeemed from the empty way of life handed down to you from your forefathers, but with the precious blood of Christ,"* (1 Peter 1:18-19). The early Christians understood that they had been bought out of slavery to sin and had been given Life in the service of the true and living God.

Now this new life is nothing other than God's life which is eternal. Thus, though *"the wages of sin is death, but the gift of God is eternal life in Christ Jesus,"* (Romans 6:23). **Redemption**, therefore, is what Jesus Christ's death is all about. It is God's saving grace, His gift of eternal life: *"For it is by grace you have been saved, through faith – and this not of yourselves, it is the gift of God – not by works, so that no one can boast."* (Ephesians 2:8-9). With the Crucifixion and Resurrection, grace takes on this unique meaning due to its unequalled provision. God comes down in Jesus Christ to move *"whoever believes in him"* to a place of eternal well-being.

> *"For God so loved the world that he gave his one and only Son, that whoever believes in him shall not perish but have eternal life."* (John 3:16)

> *"Christ Jesus... being in very nature God, did not consider equality with God something to be grasped, but* [he took] *the very nature of a servant, being made in human likeness. And*

being found in appearance as a man, he humbled himself
and became obedient to death – even death on a cross!"
(Philippians 2:5-8)

"I tell you the truth [Jesus speaking], *whoever hears my*
word and believes him who sent me has eternal life and will
not be condemned; he has crossed over from death to life."
(John 5:24)

"This is eternal life: that they may know you, the only true
God, and Jesus Christ whom you have sent." (John 17:3)

Many other biblical passages express the *"incomparable riches*
of his grace" (Ephesians 2:7), the *"indescribable gift"* (2
Corinthians 9:15). The penalty for sin (death) is gone, and people
can be moved to a place of eternal well-being.

The Alteration of Physical Death

Of course the possession of eternal life does not cancel out
physical death. Eternal life is opposed to a spiritual death state,
not the physical event. That is to say the Bible indicates we are
spiritually dead. "In Christ" we are made spiritually alive. This
changes the event of physical death for the Christian but it does
not eliminate it. Thus the New Testament speaks of believers as
"sleeping" rather than "dying" (John 11:11-14; 1 Corinthians
11:30, 15:51; 1 Thessalonians 4:15). The grace of Life transforms
death so that to the believer in Christ it is no more than sleep.

Grace then, though it does not eliminate physical death, does
something much more remarkable. It brings people out of a
spiritual death state and into a relationship with God. This
explains for me the most immediate and striking change that
occurs in the lives of people who receive God's saving grace.
They acquire a clear and unshakeable certainty that God exists.
Previously they were spiritually dead and so had no sure
conviction about God's existence. Saving grace removed that
agnosticism forever. A loving relationship with God began and

they are certain of it. With great assurance they will now tell you that God is present in their lives. Previously, you would never have heard them say anything of the sort.

I was once having a discussion with a person who thought he might be a Christian. To help clarify his condition I said, "Well then, let's go out on the streets and tell people about what great things God has done for us." He replied that he could not do this. I then gently asked why he did not think he could do it. "Is it," I ventured, "that you're not sure about God?" He admitted that this was true, and that it was the difference between us.

Here then, is the difference between the person with a truly Christian life and the person without it. One proclaims, "God knows me, and now I know Him. He loves and cares for me. He was really there all the time and deeply concerned for my well-being." The person without saving grace is not so sure about this.

Conclusion

God's grace in the Old Testament lays stress on physical ways of escape, such as from enemies, catastrophies, and fatal dangers. It points ahead to the grace that was to come from the Redeemer. Grace in the New Testament lays stress on our moral and spiritual deliverance from sin. Nevertheless, a recovery of "the old sense of sin" is essential before one sees need of God's saving grace. **Sin** is the human problem; **grace** is the remedy.

The person who feels this to be true about himself will acknowledge and express it by his actions in a sincere manner. He will have a change of mind about himself and God. There will be grief, even hatred, of sin. There will be a turning from sin to God and His service. This radical change of thought, attitude, outlook and action, is called repentance. And the Redeemer comes to those who repent of their sins (Isaiah 59:20). Obviously, this changes the direction of one's life.

This is how the truly Christian life begins, and God's saving grace gets us up and running in it. Grace takes on monumental proportions with Christ's death and resurrection. It may be foreign to a modern world. May it no longer be foreign to us.

3

Post-conversion Grace

We have been developing a fresh understanding of grace as God's loving provision that "moves people to places of well-being". The previous chapter brought to light the miraculous provision of "saving" grace: God moving people to places of **eternal** well-being. Through saving grace people are set *"free from the law of sin and death"* because Christ *"by his death... destroy*[ed] *him who holds the power of death – that is, the devil – [to] free those who all their lives were held in slavery by their fear of death,"* (Romans 8:2; Hebrew 2:14-15). Therefore, *"God demonstrates his own love for us in this: While we were still sinners, Christ died for us,"* (Romans 5:8).

Saving grace gets us up and running in God's life and gives us a glorious future when we wake up after falling asleep in Christ. The Christian life, however, is an entire life of grace right here in this life. And this means that God's grace is every day moving us into places of well-being. Let us call this "post-conversion" grace. Saving grace, then, gets us up and running in Life. Post-conversion grace keeps us running.

Righteousness

A life like this takes the pressure off, really, in the sense that it brings a lasting spiritual rest to the believer in Christ. One does "good works", but these are done out of one's love for God and others and not under the pains of trying to earn God's "favour". One rests spiritually in what has been called "the finished work of Christ".

This spiritual rest is possible because we have been declared "righteous" by God. This brings the realities of righteousness and grace into step with one another, so to speak. Again, Noah and Lot can be our examples. The Bible teaches that both men were righteous (Genesis 7:1; 2 Peter 2:8). Yet their imperfections, weaknesses and character flaws are apparent. Lot lingers before he escapes from Sodom, vacillating in unimaginable spiritual confusion. And both Noah and Lot go on benders after their ordeals are over! Their righteousness, therefore, must exist in spite of their inadequacies and extremes. How is this possible?

There is a sense in which "righteousness" is only incidentally about goodness or piety or strength of character. In the Hebrew, "righteousness" is predominately a **relationship** word, almost exactly expressed by the phrase "on the right side of". You are "right" if the judge, in terms of the law he applies, says you are so to any accusers. Now none of us have ever fulfilled God's law, and so we stand guilty of sin. Yet Jesus Christ fulfilled God's law (Matthew 5:17). Jesus, therefore, is "on the right side of" the Law. And when the Judge of all the universe declares us to be "in Christ", we are then "on the right side of" God's law and "in right relation" with Him (2 Corinthians 5:21; Galatians 2:16, 21). This is how sinners can be "justified" (just as if they had never sinned), or in the Hebrew "made right".

> *"This righteousness from God comes through faith in Christ Jesus to all who believe. There is no difference, for all have sinned and fall short of the glory of God, and are justified freely by his grace through redemption that came by Jesus Christ."* (Romans 3:22-24)

This is the legal standing before God of the believer in Jesus Christ. We therefore have not only a glorious future but a glorious present. Noah and Lot were righteous because God had said they were, and their lives were henceforth to be ruled and judged by that fact. This meant that God's grace was at work in their lives every day moving them into places of well-being. And when we are declared righteous by God, a life of post-conversion grace is ours as well in Christ. We can look with assurance to a minute by minute life of post-conversion grace. (I am adopting this term as a way to identify a large category of questions which the Christian may have in mind when picking up a book on grace.)

Sooner or later every Christian faces the fear that, "I won't be able to live the Christian life." That's right, we cannot. Just as we did not give ourselves God's life, we cannot keep ourselves up and running in it. For as it began, so it continues in grace. Post-conversion grace is vital. For the Christian who has learned its secret, there is little worry or nervousness that "I can't do it."

Thus the Bible admonishes us to *"continue in the grace of God,"* (Acts 13:43), and to be *"strong"*, *"strengthened"*, and to *"grow"* in grace (2 Timothy 2:1; Hebrews 13:9; 2 Peter 3:18). It teaches us to *"receive God's abundant provision of grace"*. (Romans 5:17). *"God"*, said the apostle Paul, *"is able to make all grace abound to you, so that in all things at all times,* [you will have] *all that you need,"* (2 Corinthians 9:8).

Animals cannot live without water. Without post-conversion grace, the Christian life suffocates. Like the farmer who receives water for irrigation from the stream that runs through his land, Christians in prayer *"approach the throne of grace with confidence, so that we may receive mercy and find grace to help us,"* (Hebrews 4:16). Having been made righteous, our lives are ruled and judged by this: receiving post-conversion grace from God.

Humility

Post-conversion grace, however, does not "come down" into a vacuum. It comes to people, and people can be uncooperative, stubborn, lacking in understanding, and even rebellious at times. So it is probably unwise for us to proceed any further without bringing in the subject of humility. After all, the Bible connects grace and humility like halves of a pair of scissors; if you only had one half you might wonder how the whole thing worked!

> *"For this is what the high and lofty One says – he who lives for ever, whose name is holy: 'I live in a high and holy place, but also with him who is contrite and lowly* [humble] *in*

21

spirit, to revive the spirit of the lowly and to revive the heart of the contrite',"   (Isaiah 57:15)

"Clothe yourselves with humility towards one another, because 'God opposes [resists] *the proud but gives grace to the humble',"*   (1 Peter 5:5)

Many other passages teach the importance of humility (Psalm 138:6; Isaiah 66:2; Philippians 2:5-8; James 4:6). Humility is easily misunderstood. It is not a certain kind of low opinion of one's talents or character. It is not, as the devil Wormwood advised his nephew Screwtape (as aspiring tempter) in C.S. Lewis' *The Screwtape Letters*, "pretty women thinking they are ugly or clever men trying to believe they are fools." Humility is about turning one's attention away from "self", to God and to one's neighbour. When one considers the will and purposes of God and the welfare of others as greater than one's own, that is humility. "Self-forgetfulness" is the way Lewis put it.

There is a kind of process here, that involves the shifting of priorities. The Bible indicates that when our regard for others becomes greater than our regard for ourselves, a certain humility, or lowliness of mind, heart or circumstance develops. This may occur when we discover that we are inferior to God and must do what He says. It may occur in the face of hardship or suffering, or doing things that we may not want to do. Obedience of this sort may spoil our hopes, pleasures, ambitions or longings. As we approach the reality of such obedience, our imagination clarifies what we are about to lose or suffer, possibly as we have never seen it before.

Let's bring this into sharp relief. The most concentrated expression of this clarification process is found in our Lord's life as described in Mark 14:32-34:

"They went to a place called Gethsemane, and Jesus said to his disciples, 'Sit here while I pray.' He took Peter, James and John along with him, and he began to be deeply distressed and troubled. 'My soul is overwhelmed with sorrow to the point of death,' he said to them."

22

Jesus had gone to pray in the Garden of Gethsemane, which in the Aramaic language means "oil press". It was just hours before His crucifixion. What lay ahead for Him was being clarified by His agony in the garden. In the passage quoted above, three Greek words in the original New Testament reveal what took place in Christ's mind. Though the words are not in the NIV rendition above, they are accurately expressed by the English words "aghast", "depressed", and "grief-stricken".

Here was Christ's passion. The unbelievable cost of Calvary clarified itself to the Suffering Servant. That Jesus did not like what He saw, in that racking oil press of lowliness, is evident from the long time He took in prayer to ask the Father if "the cup" could pass from Him. Drops of bloody sweat stained the foliage and the ground as Jesus considered and placed the importance of others as greater than himself. This comes ringing home in that climactic outburst at the end of the process, *"Not my will but Thy will be done,"* Jesus exemplified both the height and depth of realistic self-understanding before God.

The humble one comes before God and in all sincerity makes a realistic evaluation of the situation. He may say to God, "I don't understand,' or, "I don't think I can get through this, but, please God, I need more grace.' The humble one may be crushed or even bruised in some way, but never destroyed, for God comes down to move the person to a place of well-being. I realize that when your life is falling apart it will seem just the opposite, and we will come to reasons for this in later chapters. The point here is that God has promised grace to the humble to finish the course. So, strengthened by God as He comes down with grace, the suffering servant declares at some point in the process, *"Rise! Let us go,"* (Mark 14:42).

The Christian life, therefore, may fool us. It may at times require suffering or hardship. This may be physical, mental, emotional or a combination of these. We may not feel good about what lies ahead, but in facing it humbly, we will receive post-conversion grace, the loving provision of God, to get through it. True, this may not happen immediately. Outer circumstances may not change overnight. But this does not remove from reality the promise of God that Christians are destined for places of well-being. It does not matter to what depths one sinks. God's grace reached into the unfathomable depths to which our Lord sunk, which is a sign to us that He has enough grace for the shallows. As the infinite depths of Christ's descent mount up to the fullness of grace in Him, Christians have a share in both.

Pride

The opposite to humility is pride, which, incidentally, was the first of the medievalists' seven deadly sins. Pride seeks sovereignty in the human soul. It is the armour of the self-sufficient. It repels humility and therefore greatly hinders the efforts of post-conversion grace. Thus, while the lowly receive grace, the proud hit resistance.

Pride "frustrates" (Galatians 2:21 KJV) God's grace and so detours many church-goers from progressing as followers, disciples, of the Crucified One. This creates the rather anomalous category of "would-be disciples", in which the Christian life is much more theoretical than practical.

The pride of would-be disciples is "self". Would-be disciples are often willing to follow Jesus further, and they may even offer to follow Him. But when clarification breaks in on them, pride encourages them to look inward and to trust in "self" rather than in the grace of Another. At this point, joy leaks from the heart and complaints may pour from their lips like rainfall. Fellowship may diminish. God may become something of an ogre, and they have a hundred excuses.

> "As they were walking along the road, a man said to him, 'I will follow you wherever you go.'
> Jesus replied, 'Foxes have holes and birds of the air have nests, but the Son of Man has no place to lay his head.'
> He said to another man, 'Follow me.'
> But the man replied, 'Lord, first let me go and bury my father.'
> Jesus said to him, 'Let the dead bury their own dead, but you go and proclaim the kingdom of God.'

Still another said, 'I will follow you Lord; but first let me go back and say good-bye to my family.'

Jesus replied, 'No one who puts his hand to the plough and looks back is fit for service in the kingdom of God'."

This passage from Luke 9:57-62 is similar to the story of the rich young ruler, as told in Luke 18:18-23. He came to Jesus to ask what he must do to inherit eternal life. This prompted an exchange of ideas with Jesus, who told the man that he lacked one thing. *"Sell everything you have,"* Jesus said. *"Give to the poor,* [and] *then come, follow me."* Yet when he heard this, the rich ruler became very sad.

The Christian life is about following Jesus day after day, no matter where He leads us. It has everything to do with the steps we take after becoming Christians. Will we be occupied with **Jesus'** will and purposes, with **His** work, with **His** calling? If so, this means that we will humbly lose ourselves to follow Him, which will include serving others, for this is frequently where Jesus is found. It is indeed a lowly calling, but it is God calling.

Pride also encourages Christians to become enslaved by the self-help and self-potential endowments that abound today like so much dust in the wind. If so, human self-effort becomes a substitute for post-conversion grace and a means by which we try to live the Christian life. This will also occur on a much larger scale with churches and Christian organizations that trust much more in "worldly systems" for getting things done than they do in the grace of God. It has been ruefully observed that if God took His grace out of western Christianity, most Christian activity would continue anyway, because there is a kind of equivalent "world system" entrenched in the Church that has taken on a life of its own, and so runs things.

Furthermore, "self", that alpha and omega of pride, is a clinger. It does not want to give it**self** up, and pride encourages it to raise a storm of objections to the Lowly One's call, "Follow me". One person's storm may be the discovery that discipleship means attachment to a Person other than self. Another person's storm may arise when Jesus dampens the person's ardour concerning some self-effort or self-indulgence. Another storm may arise as one recognizes a barrier between himself and Jesus – a job, a proposed marriage, a broken relationship, unforgiveness, unethical behaviour. Another storm may arise at the offense of picking up one's cross and carrying it daily, for this lays the axe to self-centredness and self-determination.

Here is clarification. Discipleship cannot be reconciled to one's own initiative, said Dietrich Bonhoeffer, as if it were a career one had mapped out for himself. Man as his own centre, his own source, is offended by this. Self is miffed when it comes to relinquishing control because it strives for self-actualization.

Whenever the would-be disciple's ship hits stormy water, jumping ship is preferable to waking the Master (Luke 8:22-24). But in the storms of life, ongoing disciples seek God at the throne of grace for help in their time of need.

Continuing disciples give up self at the Cross and come to the throne of grace. They know that even if a multitude stops following Jesus, there is still no place else to go except to Him (John 6:66-69).

It is not that the others do not give up. They do give up, but in the wrong direction. Instead of giving up self to the Cross and coming to God, they give up and jump ship. The storm to produce the humility becomes the self-pity of a half-step forward but then an abrupt about-face. Rather than giving up to the grace of Another, they are offended by the "hardship" being imposed on them by this Other.

Ongoing disciples, however, know that when the going gets tough, the humble receive grace. We may not feel good about what lies ahead, but we will cooperate with God's purposes anyway. We will bow the knee before God and let Him move us through to a place of well-being. God's loving provision of grace comes, just as it did to Noah, Lot and Jesus. It may not be what we think, but it still comes. The lives of the righteous are ruled and judged by that fact.

4

Our Responsibility
to Grace

"As God's fellow workers," wrote the apostle Paul, *"we urge you not to receive God's grace in vain,"* (2 Corinthians 6:1). Here is one of several crucial biblical references to the fundamental tension between God's freely given grace and our responsibility to it. This paradox has been bristling with mixed opinions since the early days of Christendom.

Some Christians overemphasize human responsibility; others overstress the freeness of the gift. With the former there is a tendency to produce a personalized brand of religious legalism, while the latter have been known to become careless and loose morally. The first group has a kind of unspoken agreement between themselves and God that in "doing good" they add to their salvation and so will merit God's favour. The other group is largely unconcerned about their loose moral or ethical behaviour because they do not see by it any potential loss of God's favour.

Yet even the Christians who try not to get lost in the two extremes find life with such a paradox uneasy. For them, trying to live in the middle of the tension feels like walking gingerly along a very high tightrope that is stretched across an impossibly wide abyss which is miles deep. In trying to strike a balance, they find no lasting spiritual rest.

God's Initiative

I think we can relieve this nerve-racking state to some degree. Because grace engages God in "coming down", we meet face-to-face with the fact of His initiative in our lives. Apart from God's initiative, it would be impossible for us to know His will and purposes. God's initiative, therefore, immediately brings us to the question of our responsibility; that is, obedience or disobedience.

Obedience and Disobedience

Obedience and disobedience to God and their relation to grace has been the subject of much controversy throughout Church history. Even the writers of the New Testament had to address it (in particular, see Romans, Galatians and James). As mentioned above, the heart of the controversy surrounds the two extreme positions into which Christians at times swing.

Some Christians turn their obedience into a legalism by which they feel that they obtain God's grace. The apostle Paul wrote that *"After beginning with the Spirit,"* these people may be *"trying to attain* [their] *goal by human effort,"* (Galatians 3:3). If so, he goes on to say that they are placing themselves under a self-imposed law and are in danger of becoming alienated from Christ and falling away from grace (Galatians 5:4). It may be because of this that other Christians swing to the opposite extreme. Indifference to obedience leads them into a loose moral and ethical lifestyle in which they feel that grace is theirs no matter what they do. To these people, the apostle Paul wrote, *"Shall we go on sinning, so that grace may increase? By no means! Shall we sin because we are not under law but under grace? By no means!"* (Romans 6:1-2, 15).

Now a key for living restfully with this tension may be in seeing that obedience and grace, like humility and grace, have an intimacy between them. That is to say **there is a responsibility implied in the receiving of grace**. Therefore, whenever God initiates something in my life I have a responsibility to follow through on it. In other words, God's grace carries an obligation to obey. Or, if we looked at it from another direction, we could say that because God's commands are gracious (that is, for our well-being) we would be foolish not to obey.

Here, again, we can take a lesson from Noah and Lot. Apart from God's initiative, neither person would have known what was

28

going to happen **or** how to avoid it. God came down first, but then there was co-operation. Here we see their responsibility to the Ark and to the angels, that is, to the grace.

Work and Change

A related area is that obedience entails submission to another's will. And this may mean doing things according to that person's desires instead of one's own. Raise this to the will and purpose of God and it is clear that things may not always go the way we Christians want them to go (see the sub-section on humility in the previous chapter). When we perceive this, it often bogs us down and we are apt to make excuses for not following through on what God requires. We generally prefer things to remain the same or to go on without too great a shake-up. Yet we might make it easier for ourselves, here, if we were more prepared for work and change.

In some circumstances, work and change may require a lengthy task, or even one that hugs the shores of persecution. Through grace Noah obtained the Ark to ride out the storm, but the ship did not materialize out of thin air before his eyes. Some Bible scholars reckon from Genesis 6:3 that it took 120 years to build the Ark. Noah and his family of labourers must have looked peculiar to their neighbours! And there is some indication that they were ridiculed and criticized because Noah was a *"preacher of righteousness"* (2 Peter 2:5).

Clearly Noah and his family were prepared for work and change! Yes, they had the blueprint of God's purpose for them, and it was complete to the last details: the type of wood to be used, instructions for assembly, and even the boarding passes! But that is why it meant work and change; they had the grace.

Human Weakness

Some persons try to elude responsibility to grace by saying, "I'm too weak. It's just too much for me. It's too hard. I can't do it."

Obedience to God, however, is a responsibility I have regardless of my weaknesses.

A common misunderstanding here is that God is requiring me to follow through on what I cannot do. The obedience that God requires of me, however, is not that which is intrinsically impossible for me. God is no fool. He will not ask a three year old child to pilot a Boeing 747 or lift weights like a Hercules. The obedience for which I am responsible regardless of my weakness is that which God requires of me because by grace it is possible.

If I think I am likely to "fail God", I have not as yet understood the kind of provision that grace is. If I think I lack effectiveness, grace will obtain God's desired results. If I think I am too weak, good! Grace will empower me now that I have my "self" out of the way. If I feel that I am inadequate to teach a Bible class, and if God requires it, grace will sufficiently fulfil God's purpose. If I consider myself bereft of any power or authority to pray for the sick, this is humility, and God's grace will be all the capacity that both I and the person I am praying for need. If I lack moral strength to overcome a temptation, grace will empower me. If I think a certain trial or season of suffering is going to be too much for me, grace will not be insufficient.

Sure we are weak. And when we are honest with God about it, we are walking in humility. Thus grace comes, and when we are weak therefore we are strong. This may give us a clue to what the apostle Paul meant when he said, *"I will boast all the more gladly about my weaknesses, so that Christ's power may rest on me,"* (2 Corinthians 12:8-10).

The idea is to walk in humility with our weaknesses rather than allowing them to be excuses for evading our responsibilities to post-conversion grace. This means that in the long run I cannot dispute with God about grace. When Noah and Lot found grace in the eyes of the Lord, no way could they say they were not interested, not qualified, not good enough, too weak. For us, too, there will be grace when the commands arrive. And where will they arrive, except in the midst of our imperfections and weaknesses? Where else? After all, this is where we live. This is us.

Grace Swapping

Are you a shifty character? Imagine the absurdity if Lot had declared to the angels, "Good of you to warn us. I appreciate you travelling so far to get here. But I know all about grace. My grandfather, you see, used to tell me how God saved Noah and his family. So we'll just get busy building a boat." Or, imagine if Noah had somehow known about God's grace to Lot. What a foolhardy outcome if he had told God, "Well, Lord, that's good of you to warn us. But there's no way I can afford to take a century off work to go into the boat building trade. Just let me know a month or so before it starts to rain. This should give us plenty of time to round up all the animals and escape to that high mountain over there."

We may laugh, but we try it ourselves. Nevertheless, grace swapping is not optional because God has a purpose for each of us, and He knows what He is doing. Grace is not for picking and choosing. It is not a quantity of things that may be shopped for as if we were consumers seeking to outfit a house. We do not decide the size, shape or colour. This is because grace is rooted in the councils of God and the loving provision of Jesus Christ through the power of the Holy Spirit. Our responsibility is to pray and to seek godly counsel in an effort to determine what the grace of God is for us.

Now there is an interesting twist to this. We may know what God's grace is for us, but shifty characters may try to derail us from that. In the Bible, that enigma King Saul fooled around with grace swapping. One time in particular it could have led to dire consequences. Many years before he became King of Israel, the young man David was preparing to fight the Philistine giant Goliath. To slay the giant, David was trusting in the grace of God through his sling and several smooth stones. King Saul, however, decided that David was being a little naïve. He told David that he was ill-equipped for such a battle and offered him his own armour and shield in order to accomplish the feat. For a brief moment, David acquiesces and tries on Saul's armour. Immediately David's conscience starts to trouble him and he promptly disentangles himself from Saul's provision and opts for God's provision in the sling and the stones. Through this the giant was slain and the entire nation of Israel was moved to a place of well-being (1 Samuel 17).

We may not be building an Ark (I hope not!) or escaping with angels. We may not be going into battle with a slingshot and a stone. Nevertheless, we are *"labourers together with God"* (1 Corinthians 3:9 KJV). And the only way we work together with Him is by, in, and through grace. When we understand what He has called us to do, let us be careful not to swap that grace for anything.

Indecision

Another obstacle that may hinder our responsibility to grace is "indecision". In the Bible, Lot is the perfect example. Lot lingered. The grace is there, and yet he vacillates in shocking spiritual confusion. He even goes beyond hesitation. Indecision leads him to belabour a point with the angels in an attempt to evade further response to grace.

I have wondered why the dust did not fly off of Lot's feet at the command to escape for his life. Given the alternative, it seems inconceivable that he would stop to think about it. Perhaps Lot was earning a lot of money or was tied down to a few "good things" that he was unwilling to part with. He may have had certain friendships, business obligations or investments that held him back. Maybe it was social commitments or his daughters' marriages. Or it could have been that the devil held a strong grip on his heart strings. That may have been possible because this *"righteous man, living among them day after day, was tormented... by the lawless deeds he saw and heard,"* (2 Peter 2:8).

Yet whatever produced the indecision, it could not cancel the purposes of divine grace. That is what the Bible teaches us here. In the throes of his indecision, Lot suddenly remembers the secret of the righteous: they can pray for more grace.

"With the coming of dawn, the angels urged Lot, saying,

'Hurry! Take your wife and your two daughters who are here, or you will be swept away when the city is punished.' When he hesitated, the men grasped his hand and the hands of his wife and of his two daughters, and led them safely out of the city, for the Lord was merciful to them. As soon as they had brought them out, one of them said, 'Flee for your lives! Don't look back, and don't stop anywhere in the plain! Flee to the mountains or you will be swept away!' But Lot said to them, 'No, my lord, please! Your servant has found grace in your eyes, and you have shown great kindness to me in sparing my life. But I can't flee to the mountains; this disaster will overtake me, and I'll die. Look, here is a town near enough to run to, and it is small. Let me flee to it – it is very small, isn't it? Then my life will be spared.' He said to him, 'Very well, I will grant this request too; I will not overthrow the town you speak of. But flee there quickly, because I cannot do anything until you reach it'."

(Genesis 19:15-22)

This is the secret of the righteous. We may come boldly before the throne of grace to obtain mercy and to receive help in our time of need (Hebrews 4:16). Obstacles of "the next step" vanish. The lives of the righteous are ruled and judged by this fact.

5

Person-to-Person
Grace Giving

If we were to give them a theme, the previous chapters are about grace straight from God to people. But this is not the end of the story. There is also the biblical theme of grace giving among people themselves. So as there is grace from God-to-Man, there is person-to-person grace giving. Here are several of the many biblical stories that highlight this.

When it was time for the patriarch Jacob (renamed Israel) to die, he called his youngest son, Joseph, to his side and said to him, *"If I have found **grace** in your eyes... do not bury me in Egypt... carry me out of Egypt and bury me where* [my fathers] *are buried,"* (Genesis 47:29-30). Jacob longed for burial in the "promised land" of Canaan. But because there had been a long, devastating famine in Canaan, Jacob had moved his large family to Egypt, where he had been living for years. His insistence for burial in Canaan showed his faith in God's promise to him that the nation of Israel would be established in Canaan. Jacob would rather be identified with his nation in death, and not the nation of Egypt. It was an act of grace from Joseph to secure this for Jacob.

In the book of Numbers, grace played a part in dividing up the land of Canaan among Israel's twelve tribes. When the offspring of Israel's sons Reuben and Gad approach Moses to grant them a portion of land suitable for cattle, they say, *"If we have found **grace** in your eyes, let this land* [east of the Jordan river] *be given* [us] *as our possession,"* (Numbers 32:5). And Moses gave that grace.

In the book of Ruth, Boaz, a prominent land owner, has singled out the young widow Ruth to receive certain gifts. Ruth recognizes these gifts for what they are and says to Boaz, *"Why* *have I found such **grace** in your eyes?"* (Ruth 2:10).

Person-to person grace giving is also found throughout David and Jonathan's relationship. During the years preceding his enthronement as king of Israel, David continually faces the rather aggravating and exhausting strain of trying to keep one step ahead of being skewered by King Saul's spear. Even though Jonathan is Saul's son, Jonathan befriends David and helps him to escape Saul's wrath several times. David recognizes the nature of this help and says to Jonathan, *"Your father knows very well that I have found **grace** in your eyes,"* (1 Samuel 20:3).

Giving Grace Today

Here are several principles of person-to-person grace giving that may help us update what the Bible teaches, to our activities today.

Be willing to get involved. This is where the sacrificial aspect of giving grace may be offensive and unattractive to us. Person-to-person grace giving challenges us with its often stark, down-to-earth applications. It may mean getting active in other people's lives much more purposefully than we may at first be willing to do. Here, then, is the sacrificial character of grace.

Beware of the welfare trap. In some situations where we might be able to help, it is tempting to think it does not matter if we pitch in to give grace; for example, to the poor and the needy. As the thinking goes, I pay taxes, so let the State assist the poor with unemployment benefits, dole and other welfare assistance programmes. We must be careful about this attitude; it can produce paralysis of grace giving. We tend to look the other way when in the presence of the poor and the needy. We withhold.

Yet giving that is grace, takes risks with the poor, the needy, the down-and-out, the unknown. In fact, one of the characteristics of God's grace is that it is given most freely to such people. What was it that God told the nation Israel? To paraphrase, He did not choose them or set His affection on them because they were something special (Deuteronomy 7:7). This choice of the unknown to receive a blessing was also behind God's appointment of David to be Israel's second king, which even

36

fooled one of God's prophets! (1 Samuel 16:1-13). Think, too, about God's risk in choosing the Rabbi Saul, a persecutor of Christians, to become a Christian apostle. And what about God's choice of **us**? *"Think of what you were when you were called. Not many of you were wise by human standards; not many were influential; not many were of noble birth. But God chose the foolish... the weak... the lowly... the despised,"* (1 Corinthians 1:26-29).

Develop spiritual eyesight. People who do not have perfect vision may wish that they did. But none of us needs perfect optical vision in order to give grace. We simply need to be able to see in a special way; let us say a spiritual way.

In more than 90% of the Old Testament passages that use the word "grace", the words "eyes" or "sight" also appear. Whatever else this may mean, it suggests that in order to give grace we must first have seen the need. Seeing needs, however, is not usually what prevents us from giving today. The dilemma is that what we are seeing is too overwhelming. We find ourselves dwarfed by seeing what is far beyond our capacity to alleviate. Too many needs exist, and they are too immense. As a result, we tend to think that our little contribution cannot possibly make any difference. This may lead us to shut down our compassion and inhibit us from giving grace. Jesus, however, has not cancelled the commands to love one another and to be a Good Samaritan because the odds are stacked against us.

The way to break free from this kind of grace paralysis is to cultivate the knack of seeing the needs we can do something to alleviate. **Spiritual** vision focuses its grace telescope on the people it knows it can help.

Take inventory. Getting ready to give like this first means taking inventory to see what we possess and how some of it may become grace for others. Joseph, Boaz and Jonathan, for example, knew that they had the resources to give the kinds of grace that they did. The most profound expression of person-to-person grace giving that I am aware of took place in the early Church shortly after Pentecost: *"No one claimed that any of his possessions was his own, but they shared everything they had. There were no needy persons among them,"* (Acts 4:32-34). The King James version says that *"great grace"* was with them!

What, then, do we have that we may want to give as grace? How about skills, resources, assets, possessions, talents? Some Christians have **time**. If we find ourselves with time on our hands, we may want to consider donating some of that time as grace. How about giving a few hours of time each week to assist a charity organization? How about visiting the sick or widows? A former athlete could take some time to befriend a restless youth. A childless couple could give some time to help out at a "children's club".

Some Christians are unemployed. They may have a lot of time to give. It may be time, therefore, to prayerfully consider going into volunteer work for a season. I once did full-time volunteer work in the inner-city of Detroit, Michigan, and it was a very rewarding experience. It was fifteen years ago, but I am still walking in the grace of God which came to me that year as I reached out to others with grace.

Occasionally we need **to make time** for grace giving. Tim (not his real name) was driving to an appointment when he passed an apartment building and saw people gathering around an elderly man who was lying unconscious on the ground. Seeing no one tending to the man, Tim parked his car and ran over to see what he could do. Upon discovering that the man had had a heart attack and that an ambulance was on its way, Tim bent down next to the man and began to pray. When the ambulance arrived, the small crowd dispersed. The man was left utterly alone with the medics. No one seemed to want to get involved.

Tim got permission from the medics to meet them at the hospital. He knew that this would make him quite late for his appointment; he might even miss it. But he had been thinking that the heart attack victim might need someone at the hospital to serve him in some way, even if he did not regain consciousness.

The cardiac team did revive the man, just about the time a few family members arrived. Though they were shaken by what had happened, some of the shock was relieved when they talked to Tim and discovered that he had stood by their father to offer what help he could. In the ensuing conversation, the family also discovered that Tim was a Christian and that he had been praying for their father. Now this family was part of a culture that had a bad image of Christians. Tim believes that the grace of time and prayer brought a redemptive element into that family, which dispelled their caricature of Christianity. As he drove away, Tim realised that some appointments are not scheduled on the calendar!

Other Christians have skills or resources that could be given as grace. Even after a tiring week's work a nurse or a physiotherapist may want to provide occasional care or therapy for a disabled neighbour. Other professionals (doctors, dentists, technicians) may want to use their holiday time to serve in short-time missions contexts. As a person who has writing and editorial skills, I have given them at times in service freely to people and to one mission's organization in particular. Others may have skills or talents in music, cooking, gardening, teaching, mechanics, carpentry, computers, mothering and so forth, which could be turned into freely given grace.

The list is long, and the possibilities are only limited to how much we hold back. Take inventory and try to think of ways in which to use your time, skills, resources and talents in the context of grace giving. I can assure you that when you give grace, burdens will be lifted off people and their faces will light up. Lives will be changed as you move them to places of well-being. They may even ask, "Why have I found grace in your sight?"

Of course, this may entail immersing ourselves in the lives of others much more realistically than we may have thought. Here, then, is the struggle between our values and the sacrificial values of God's kingdom. Practically, this may mean re-scheduling our time, re-arranging our priorities. Some social activities may have to be dropped. Some evenings may have to be freed up. Hours of needless talking on the telephone, or drifting around shopping, may have to be cut back. Listless hours spent wandering around the neighbourhood may have to become more focused and productive.

Now there is no charge for person-to-person grace giving, for if it is grace, it is freely given.

Financial Grace

Another kind of person-to-person grace giving may be more difficult. There is an irksome side to the Christian life that is often downplayed, and that is the teaching of the Bible about money. Jesus' teaching is particularly severe. Someone has noted that the tendency is to tone down Jesus' criticism about money because it flies in the face of virtually everything we have been taught about it from our cultures. But there you have it, *"No servant can serve two masters. Either he will hate the one and love the other, or he will be devoted to the one and despise the other. You cannot serve both God and Money,"* (Luke 16:13).

Was Jesus exaggerating? Yet someone will say, "I don't have a problem here. I pay my tithes." If so, that is good. But people who pay tithes usually do so because they believe it is something they owe God and the Church. I would kindly like to suggest that that is not financial grace giving; it's payment. One feels it is owed, that it is required giving. Financial grace giving, like all other kinds of grace giving, is not giving that is owed or somehow earned by the recipient. It is a free gift.

Another person may say, "But I can't give like that. I just don't have the money." This may be true. But it may also be true that that is merely a polite alibi to hold back financial grace as money we would rather spend on ourselves. If so, we may want to rearrange the way we spend our money. This may mean getting out of debt, or fighting off the temptation to buy unnecessary items, or resisting the advertising industry, or making modest purchases instead of being impulsive or extravagant in our spending. Savings' strategies like these may help a Christian to say, "I **do** have the money to give!"

The idea here is to create an available flow of cash that can be used strictly as financial grace. If we cut back on expenditures, we could place the money we were going to spend into a "financial grace savings account". This would not be "savings" that stockpile. It would be a way to keep ready cash flowing in and out as financial grace.

I would also like to suggest that in giving financial grace we stop seeing through the eyes of the big charity bandwagon organizations and campaigns. Having lived on the mission field for several years, I saw first-hand how this detracts significantly from the financial support of thousands of missionaries who do not have the commercial hype, the media advertisers or the television slot by which to raise money for their work. We tend to give to those projects that are well-known because they are well-advertised. As a result, seasoned missionaries struggle unnecessarily financially. They are a blind spot in our thinking. We are not accustomed to "seeing" them. And they remain largely unsupported.

Approachableness

Sometimes when we try to give grace we encounter a kind of rebuff from the potential receiver. Cultivating an attitude of "approachableness" in the presence of the needy may help them to be more receptive to our grace overtures. The needy have a sort of radar that turns them off to some people and on to others. Christians ought to be those they turn on to.

We can become approachable by appearing friendly and not so tightly organized. We do not want to appear to be so preoccupied with other things that we seem disinterested when we are in the presence of someone we are trying to help. In appearing cold and mechanical, we may seem impersonal and so cut off the needy's access to us.

I have a friend whose large house has a slightly frayed look to it! Yet it is known throughout his community as being open to the needy. One day someone said to him, "You're stupid. If someone just turned up at my door wanting a bed like that, I'd tell them to go to the police station!" To this my friend replied, "Don't worry, they never will. The needy have instincts."

It is difficult to count how many people this family has sheltered and helped over the years because their home was "approachable". Many of these persons became Christians while staying in their home. The other man was having difficulty in "seeing".

Giving grace to strangers is more difficult than giving it to friends or family. The latter are already in our lives. Not so the former. "Approachableness" will let us attract these shooting stars so that they may become newly orbiting acquaintances whose lives we may grace.

Marie used "listening" to make herself approachable to Cathy. When Marie saw Cathy for the first time, Cathy was walking near a church and seemed confused. As the two began to talk, Marie realised that Cathy was both physically and emotionally needy. Further contact between them led to a lot of listening on Marie's part. This helped Cathy start to unload herself emotionally. A friendship began to develop and Marie occasionally invited Cathy into her home for meals and to play with the children. This, too, was therapeutic for Cathy, who, in turn, began to trust Marie and listen to her advice. This eventually resulted in some remediation of Cathy's physical and emotional needs. In Marie, a busy wife and mother, Cathy found a grace giver. She had only the State before.

Conclusion

A lot of noise is being made today that we need to be "global Christians". I wonder if we are puzzled about this because we have not yet understood and obeyed our Lord's command to be "neighbourhood Christians"? This is what it means to give grace from person-to-person. It is to have the right kind of eyesight, to take inventory, to assess how we may give and to make ourselves approachable. Jesus Christ did this as He stretched out His arms to die on Calvary's cross. This is a high calling, but it is God calling. And it leaves one to answer the question, "Has anyone found grace in my sight?"

6

Spiritual
Grace Giving

In this chapter we will discuss "spiritual gifts" and their relation to God's grace. But first, in an effort to steer clear of a serious error, something must be said about the use of the word "spiritual".

When the word "spiritual" enters a discussion, the temptation is to think, "Now we're really going to get to the spiritual stuff. Now we're going to learn what it means to be spiritual." Thinking like this is a mistake. It eventually creates a kind of dualism in our minds whereby Christians become pitted against one another as "more spiritual" and "less spiritual". This results from placing false values on the types of work done by Christians.

For example, pastors and missionaries are often seen as more spiritual than brothers and sisters in Christ who run farms, raise families, or work in shops. Thus we tend to say that pastors and missionaries are doing "Christian" work, while the others are unfortunately stuck with "regular" jobs. If they could get into "Christian" work, then we tend to think that they would be more spiritual.

The Bible, however, knows nothing of such a dualism between the "more" or the "less" spiritual Christians. The distinction the Bible makes is between the obedient and the disobedient, not between the more or less spiritual. For God judges us not by **how** spiritual we are but in **what** we are doing with the grace He gives us. The term "spiritual gifts", therefore, is merely a way of describing a special kind of person-to-person grace giving. Perhaps it could be described as Person-to-person-to-person grace giving, for reasons that will soon become obvious. But it must not be thought of as a way of describing "more spiritual" Christians.

God's Gifts to the Church

After our Lord's resurrection and ascension into heaven, the Holy Spirit was sent to the disciples at Pentecost. He came laden with gifts for Christ's Church, and He has been giving gifts to the Church ever since. The Church, of course, is made up of individual Christians, who are the recipients of the gifts.

For example, certain men are gifts to the Church: apostles, prophets, evangelists, pastors and teachers (Ephesians 4:7-12). Romans 12:3-8 lists seven gifts, which are frequently called "motivational gifts": prophesying, teaching, encouraging, serving, contributing, leadership and showing mercy.[1] These are frequently divided into two groups. The first three being "speaking gifts", the latter four being "serving gifts". First Corinthians 12:1-11 lists nine gifts that are usually called "spiritual gifts": wisdom, knowledge, faith, healing, miraculous powers, prophecy, distinguishing between spirits, speaking in different kinds of tongues and the interpretation of tongues. And theologians have identified many other gifts in the New Testament as well.

This is not the book to discuss all the characteristics of these gifts. Here we want to stick to the subject of this book and see these gifts in relation to God's grace.

The Nature of the Gifts

It is unfortunate that in English translations of the New Testament the affinity between God's gifts and His grace is not as clear as it is in the original Greek. For example, in Romans 12:6 we read, *"We have different gifts, according to the grace given us."* And in 1 Peter 4:10, *"Each one should use whatever gift he has to serve others, faithfully administering God's grace in its various forms."* In the Greek, however, the intimacy between "grace" and "gifts" is striking.

Charis is the Greek word in the New Testament for "grace". And the most frequently used Greek word for "gifts" is simply formed by adding the suffix "ma" to **charis** to make **charisma**.

Thus, *"We have different **charisma**, according to the **charis** given us."* And, *"Each one should use whatever **charisma** he has to serve others, faithfully administering God's **charis** in its various forms."* It's a kind of play on words. There is no **charisma** without **charis**. The latter gives birth to the former. Without **charis** (grace) we would have no **charisma** (gifts).

Viewed this way, it seems umistakably clear that this should heal one of the most damaging rifts within Christendom: the snubbing, alienation and lack of dialogue that can be a way of life between so-called **charis**matics and non**charis**matics. The dismissiveness and icy feelings between the two groups is a dangerous judgementalism. We do not find the charismatic/noncharismatic distinction in the Bible, for it implies that part of Christ's Church is without **charis**. Let us be wise. The New Testament teaches that **every Christian has charisma**.

The Stewardship Question

The point of the apostles' Peter and Paul is not to create a charismatic/noncharismatic distinction but to exhort all Christians to be good stewards of God's **charis** with their **charisma**. Therefore, concerning "spiritual" gifts the Bible exhorts all Christians as **stewards of charis** (grace). The strength of this comes through in the above passage in First Peter in the King James Version, which admonishes us to "minister" the gifts to one another *"as good stewards of the manifold grace (charis) of God."* All Christians, therefore, have a responsibility to God's "spiritual" gifts just as they do with other grace. And that responsibility is to be a good steward. Stewards manage another person's property. **Charisma** is the "property" of God that He has given us in the nature of grace to manage. Can we manage that?

God's grace gifts to Christians are used in the power of the Holy Spirit to build up Christ's Church, which is His body (Ephesians 4:1-16; 1 Corinthians 12-14; Romans 12:3-13). Through these gifts, God has made sure that nothing for His Son's Church is lacking. When these gifts are used they edify, build up, strengthen and heal Christ's body.

Now there is an intimacy between God and the Christian here that we must not miss. These are God's gifts, and whenever they are being expressed by Christians, God is specially present in that moment, which is the only reason they could be expressed. When a pastor pastors, or when a Christian prays for the sick or expresses a message of wisdom or shows God's mercy (and so forth), he is exercising a gift in which God Himself is present with grace for the recipient. The gift "comes down" from God to and through the Christian to the recipient. Here, then, is Person-to-person-to-person grace giving. And it carries that fundamental idea of grace: the moving to well-being.

This is why we face that all-important question of our stewardship, or management, of these grace gifts. Stewards manage another person's property either carelessly or carefully. And too often, instead of moving one another into places of well-being by use of the gifts, we quarrel, alienate and hurt one another because of them.

Releasing the Potential of Spiritual Gifts

It is possible, however, to ease the tensions surrounding the gifts, so that we might find biblical ways of living in unity with each other in the midst of a diversity of understanding and expression of the gifts. I believe this is possible because I have seen it happen. And when it does, it means that we are being better stewards of grace. Let's look, therefore, at ways in which we can untie several knots in the glorious potential of grace-giftedness.

Start with an AID's test. "Spiritual gifts" is one of the most ignitable issues within Christendom. Yet there is nothing wrong with the gifts themselves, as if something were faulty with God's design. **Charisma** is sent to us from our Father and is *"good and perfect,"* (James 1:17). The ensuing explosions surrounding these gifts, then, cannot be traced back to defects in them. Rather, it may be the short fuse we bring to them. And that short fuse may be our attitude. If our attitude is not that of **grace**, when the dust settles over our word wars, all we will have succeeded in doing is to have tied knots in the potential of the gifts.

We may need to take an Attitude Inspection and Discernment test. There is a very real sense in which the attitudes of Christians act as the power of a fulcrum to unite or divide the body of Christ. Thus one's attitude towards grace-giftedness has a decisive influence as to whether there is harmony or discord, a building up or a tearing down, amongst Christians.

Rethink our theology. If we think that we have "the right" or "the only" theology about God's grace gifts, we may be causing division about the gifts. It could be that in clinging so tightly to "the right" theology we have ended up with an improper theology.

As odd as it may seem, we may be able to untie this knot in the potential by developing an appreciation for "mystery". We live in an age in which science and technology want everything to be explained. The Church has picked up this kind of thinking and aimed it at God. Be that as it may, there will always remain an air of mystery about God, and by inference those things which are His.

Grace-giftedness is a case in point. Much puzzles us about them. They are at times baffling. We have unanswered questions, and many will remain unanswered. It is not possible, therefore, to draw an air-tight theology from the Bible about God's grace gifts because an intrinsic other-worldliness surrounds them. They are God's. The inspired men who gave us the New Testament understood this and do not attempt to have a final say in the matter.

This is not to suggest, however, that no biblical guidelines are given. But it's an interesting thing, this. For the guidelines are not so much about the gifts as they are for the gifted. The only absolute rule, and it is the first one, is that God's grace gifts are given only to Christians. After that has been established, some characteristics of the gifts are listed in Scripture. But that is about it, as far as the gifts themselves. The dominant guidelines are then aimed at the gifted, **all** Christians.

The heart of these guidelines is the command to live in humility and brotherly love amongst ourselves. This, for instance, is the dominant message of First Corinthians 12-14. The apostle is wisely nailing down believers to humility and brotherly love towards one another while allowing grace-giftedness a free flow in a wide variety of expressions.

"And now I will show you the most excellent way," states the preface to First Corinthians 13. And what follows is not a polished theology about spiritual gifts but a lengthy and heart-felt command to genuine love among the diversely gifted. This love esteems others above self (humility), and it accepts others because it recognizes that the whole thing is all of grace. We acknowledge that we are undeserving and without strength and no better than other members of Christ's Body. What is left, then, other than expressing and giving grace freely among ourselves?

We are a Body, not busy-bodies. As a Body, we express the harmony-in-uniqueness that is Christ's Church. And we do this even when grace giftedness is strongly contrasted among believers, churches and denominations. This is indeed a great mystery. But it is no reason to knot the potential.

Be flexible. Sometimes we evade being good stewards of grace-giftedness because expressing the gifts may either be disagreeable to us, or take us outside the limits of our normal use of them. If so, we may be somewhat inflexible. Nevertheless, there is a kind of divine pliability to God's grace gifts.

As a general rule, Christians cannot make the excuse I used to hear in the union shop where I once worked. There, workers could say, "It's not my classification". By this they could evade doing any work outside their normal job descriptions whenever the foreman might ask them to. In extreme cases, this attitude has been known to shut down assembly lines and entire shops!

Christians know no such luxury. There is a kind of divine pliability with God in the area of grace-giftedness. This makes it possible, should the need arise, for us to serve outside our "classifications". When we know what our unique giftings are, the temptation is to get locked into them alone. This may become a subtle means by which to evade the all-inclusive demands of Christian duty, service, love, mercy, proclamation of the Gospel and so forth, which may take us at times much further afield than our "classifications".

I may never have taught a Bible class, or practised evangelization, or cast out a demon, or prayed for the sick. I may think, I'm not "qualified". That's right, I'm not qualified for this life of grace. I'm not even qualified to express God's spiritual gifts in the areas that I am used to. It's all of grace. I merely co-operate with God. If God, therefore, wants to reach out to move one of His children to a place of well-being through me, and if He wants to do this in a way I am not used to, no way can I say I'm not qualified, not good enough, not ready. (Where have we heard this before?) I merely need to humble myself and become a responsible steward to the "new" grace, just as I have been doing to the more familiar grace. I merely need to co-operate with the grace He will bring in that moment. As He comes down with grace for the spiritual gifts that I am familiar with expressing, so, too, He will come down with grace for me to fulfil what He requires of me outside of my "classifications"

A splendid example of this divine pliability and human flexibility is found in the book of Nehemiah. The nation of Israel had been in captivity and exile in Babylon but the Babylonian Empire had been overthrown by the Medes and Persians. So Cyrus, the Persian king, permitted thousands of Israelites to return to Jerusalem in their homeland. Once there, they rebuilt their temple, as recorded in the book of Ezra. But the wall of the city Jerusalem was still in ruins, and it was under Nehemiah's leadership that the wall was rebuilt.

Under Nehemiah's leadership we see a marvellous expression of human flexibility and adaptability to God's grace in this situation. Persons who were "graced" by God to be priests, goldsmiths, perfume makers, local politicians, wives, mothers, temple servants, merchants and so forth set aside their "classifications" to serve as carpenters, stone masons, labourers, sentinels, soldiers, cooks, blacksmiths, errand runners and the like. Nehemiah Chapter Three reverberates with the drama. God has given the word to get the wall rebuilt, and as He is providing grace for that, men and women must work alongside one another outside of their "classifications" to fulfil God's purpose. Of course, Christians are not called to build walls, but to build up one another, which may mean more flexibility about the grace gifts.

Appreciate diversity. God's House. A holy Temple. Christ's Body. These are metaphors in the New Testament for the

Christian Church (1 Corinthians 3:16; 6:19; Ephesians 2:19; Colossians 1:18; 1 Corinthians 12-14). Now "difference" is essential to a properly functioning house, temple or body; especially "body". Each image, therefore, conveys an entity that is simultaneously heterogeneous **and** one. Here, then, is God's approval of a Church that is uniquely contrasted among its members. This brings us to the over-arching miracle of grace-giftedness: we can be more fully individuals while being more closely at one.

A prism is a fascinating object. Held in the sunlight it refracts that light into many coloured lights which shine reflected throughout the room. As the source of the multicolours is one light, so, too, with spiritual gifts. God is the unifying Source of His grace's refraction – distribution – into many giftings and their subsequent reflections – expressions – throughout Christ's Church. Through this miracle Jesus sends His many-coloured "lights" both into His Church and out into the world (Matthew 5:14). An appreciation for Christian diversity (sin and heresy aside) may help us to become more at one, and so build up Christ's body as a united witness to a watching world.

This, it seems to me, is what Jesus meant when He prayed in John 17, *"that all of them* [those who believe in him] *may be one, Father... That they may be one as we are one... to let the world know,"* (vs. 21-23). There is a lot of noise being made today in the so-called New Age community about "unity-in-diversity". Despite any good intentions here, "New Age" councils and agendas to promote unity-in-diversity will have the equivalent result of chasing down a desert mirage. It is Christ's Church that is the unimpeachable witness of humanity redeemed and reunited harmoniously within its diversity. It is not any other institution but Christ's Church which is the proof that one after another, as someone has said, the barriers separating man from God and from one another are removed until nothing remains to disfellowship people from one another or to hide God's face from them.

That is what it means to *"reach unity in the faith"*, to *"become mature"*, to *"attaining to the whole measure of the fullness of Christ."* (Ephesians 4:13). What is left, then, except to worship with the apostle Paul, *"Oh, the depth of the riches of the wisdom and knowledge of God!"* (Romans 11:33).

.

[1]Briefly, the gifts listed in Romans 12:3-8 have been called "motivational" because they seem to indicate either strong desires to work in the Church in certain ways or strong natural inclinations to do particular kinds of work. For example, some Christians find that they are "mercy oriented", and it is easy for them to show mercy. Others find it "natural" to teach. Others will have tendencies to serve quietly behind-the-scenes. In the teaching that I have heard on the subject, it is thought that all Christians can identify themselves primarily with one of these "motivational" characteristics, though some Christians notice two or three that are fairly strong in their lives.

7

New
Realities

The previous chapter concluded with the rather pleasant sensation that the transforming power of grace moves us into new realities. This is the sure hope of all Christians, even to the suffering. We do not remain forever in the same situations and conditions. God comes down to move us into places of well-being. And He does this both inwardly and outwardly in our lives.

New Inner Realities

A.W. Tozer, an insightful Christian minister, wrote that the whole purpose of God in redemption is to make us holy and restore us to the image of God. Here is the grace of God at work within the soul, transforming the inner man, the interior life, into Christlikeness. This moves the ongoing disciple into increasing levels or degrees of inner well-being. One's character becomes more like Jesus Christ's.

The Bible uses the metonymy "heart" to speak of the inner man, the interior life, the inner conditions which shape character. And when the Bible speaks of "the heart", it carries the predominant idea of motivation and intent, or the central direction of our desires, interests and activities.

When I was a child, I occasionally heard the phrase, "deepest, darkest Africa". I'm not sure what the media meant by that, but it does seem somewhat analogous to the human heart. When we come to God for redemption, we come with a whole host of sinful "character"istics that defile the inner life and ruin the image of God in us. When we come to God, we come just as we are, with proud, stony, faithless, jealous, deceitful hearts. And when we come to God in humility, He comes to us with post-conversion grace to transform even the deepest, darkest hearts. Through the transforming power of grace, the proud heart becomes humble, the stony fleshly, the faithless faithful, the jealous trusting, the deceitful true. The interior life takes on new characteristics of Christlikeness, which begin to form and grow within us like pleasant fruit.

The apostle Peter goes so far as to say that inner transformation confirms, ratifies and strengthens our Christianity:

> *"Therefore, my brothers, be all the more eager to make your calling and election sure. For if you do **these things**, you will never fall, and you will receive a rich welcome into the eternal kingdom of our Lord and Saviour Jesus Christ."*
>
> (2 Peter 1:10-11)

The question, then, is what are "these things" to which Peter refers? The answer is found in the preceding verses, five through seven, which list seven Christlike characteristics that we are to add to our faith in God. This again brings us to the thought of our responsibilities. The seven qualities are: goodness (virtue), knowledge, self-control (temperance), perseverance (patience), godliness, brotherly love and love.

If we *"make every effort to add* [these things] *to* [our] *faith,"* Peter writes, *"if* [we] *possess these qualities in increasing measure, they will keep* [us] *from being ineffective and unproductive in* [the] *knowledge of our Lord Jesus Christ. But if anyone does not have them, he is short-sighted and blind, and has forgotten that he has been cleansed from his past sins,"* (2 Peter 1:5, 8-9).

Selfishness, pride, bitterness, envy, cruelty, lust, vindictiveness, hatred, sarcasm, covetousness, cowardliness, laziness and other interior ills index fallen man's characteristics. These are noticeably different than those of the Master's love, joy, peace, patience, kindness, goodness, faithfulness, gentleness, self-control, honesty, humility, generosity, forgiveness and other *"fruit of the Spirit,"* (Galatians 5:22-23; Colossians 3:12-14). Through post-conversion grace, God comes down to do a little soul surgery to give us the godly characteristics of a new heart.

> *"I will sprinkle clean water on you, and you will be clean; I will cleanse you from all your impurities and from all your idols. I will give you a new heart and put a new spirit in you; I will remove from you your heart of stone and give you a heart of flesh. And I will put my Spirit in you and **move you** to follow my decrees and be careful to keep my laws."*
>
> (Ezekiel 36:25-27)

Nevertheless, resistance to the transforming power of grace on the heart is not uncommon. We often are quite comfortable living with certain "old familiar friends": sickening habits, selfish ambitions, childish failings, holding on to what is questionable and so forth. All of us have our own peculiar sins, faults, failures, temptations, struggles, blind spots, misplaced footfalls and residual worldly habits that post-conversion grace within the soul seeks to transform. This is a life-long process, and through it the image of God in us is restored and new inner realities of well-being, peace, contentment and moral and spiritual strength become ours. God has set His heart to come to us to move us from root problems to the root of the righteous, from habitual stumblings to the Rock on which we will stand, from a lack of faith to pure love, from a vain mouth to a tongue whose words are as choice as silver, from self-centredness to laying down our lives for others, from fear of man to holy boldness, from striking back to turning the other cheek, from unwillingness to serve to going the extra mile, from bitterness to forgiveness. This, and so much more.

Though at times it may be difficult to submit to grace for a change, great joy and assurance await Christians who cooperate with the work of post-conversion grace in their hearts. God will come down earnestly with loving provisions of grace, in so many ways, day in and day out, to be with us even in the most depressing circumstances, trials or sufferings. This He will do to move us to places of inner well-being. Outer circumstances may not change immediately but the character of our Lord gets formed within us, and we shall stand one day in a practical holiness shining like the stars.

New Outer Realities

If we look again to Genesis, it is clear the grace quite literally released Noah and Lot into new outer realities. This blessing holds true for us as well. Yet at times, like Noah and Lot, it can be quite demanding or disheartening waiting for the new. One starts to wonder, to question, to doubt what is going on, what one is hoping for.

This came ringing home to me many years ago. I was a young Christian, and I worked in an automobile dealership selling car parts. I had been employed there fore two years. I liked the job and thought I would be working there for many more years. And due to much extra effort, I was occasionally rewarded with raises in pay. Yet without warning at the beginning of the third year my employer slashed my earnings by twenty percent!

Of course, I immediately took this as an indication from God that I was to get another job. I was very upset, but I began looking for another job, and within a couple of weeks I had two new jobs offered to me. The only thing that remained, then, was to pray about which job to take. But when I prayed, it shocked me to realize that God was telling me not to quit my job and to keep working there.

"But, God," I moaned, "I'm perfectly justified to get another job. Look what's happened!"

"Yes," He replied, "you may have a right to have another job, but you have a greater responsibility to me."

I knew that to take another job would be disobedience, and somehow I made the decision to stay. Afterwards, it occurred to me that following Jesus sometimes means moving **down** the economic ladder. I then began to pray to discover **when** I could leave and get another job. But God was silent about this. And to make matters worse, my circumstances at work got worse month after month. Eventually a year passed, and still God was silent about releasing me into something new. And then suddenly it happened. I received an unsolicited phone call from a friend who knew where I could get a very good job. When I prayed, God said, "This is it." A week later I was released into a new outer reality. I began work at another car dealership, and it became one of the best jobs I have ever had.

Consolation for Sufferers

I would like to close this booklet in a special way, by speaking to those who are in pain or suffering of some kind. New inner and outer realities are part of the life of grace even for you.

We can look to our Lord as the Supreme Example of this. It does not often occur to us that Jesus Christ lived a life of grace. We realize that God has grace for us, but we may not recognize that God had grace for Jesus. Jesus Christ's birth, mission, miracles, accomplishments, teachings, travels, pain, suffering, death and resurrection were all part of a life of grace. We frequently look to Jesus as our example for service (John 13:15), for submission (Luke 22:42), for suffering (1 Peter 2:21), for supplication (Mark 6:46), or for sacrifice (Philippians 2:5-8). Yet we can also look to Jesus as our model for grace.

For example, we have already spoken of Gethsemane, that racking oil-press of intellectual and emotional torture. It was grace that moved the man Christ Jesus through this and out of it into a new reality. A remarkable passage in Philippians 2:9 (RSV) reveals that grace which *"bestowed on Jesus the name which is above every name..."*. "Bestowed", here, is εχαρισατο (echarisato), which is from χαρισ (charis), that is, grace. Jesus by His life and death did not earn it or achieve it. It was freely given to Him by **grace**. Even Jesus was "saved by grace"!

What an amazing hope for sufferers. Yet what we must understand, here, is grace is the fountainhead of hope. Just as we have seen the intimacy between grace and humility, and obedience and righteousness, so, too, there is intimacy between grace and hope. Thus, the person with God's grace is the person who walks in hope.

Let's unpack this truth and bring it into the light. We have already noted that **charis**, the New Testament word for "grace", is the source of our spiritual gifts. Yet another essential idea surrounding the word **charis** is that of "a divine outlook on life." That is to say **charis** (grace) produces in Christians a divine outlook, an unfailing future perspective. In a word, hope. This is a characteristic of grace.

Now to say "unfailing" is not to say "unwavering". At times, we walk among dimly lit hopes. And even a full eclipse of hope is not uncommon. Yet even during an eclipse of hope, the Christian still lives a life of grace, which means that hope will return. It cannot be permanently extinguished precisely because of grace.

The most stunning encouragement we can take from this is found in our Lord's life (of grace) from the point of view of Psalm 22. This is that graphic passage depicting the Suffering Servant's extreme physical agony and crushing emotional anguish, as it portrays the crucifixion with disturbing clarity and a revelation of the fullest ever eclipse of hope.

The Psalm opens with our Lord's cry on the Cross, *"My God, my God, why have you forsaken me?"* (Matthew 27:46; Mark 15:34). What follows this for the next twenty verses is the sufferer's descent to rock bottom despair. Abandonment by God. There is no hope. The eclipse is full.

And, yet, Jesus did not only live by grace. He also *"suffered death... by the grace of God,"* (Hebrews 2:9). Now it is not possible to live or die (and we die many little deaths daily) by grace and to **remain** without hope. For the Christian, hope is not the I-hope-so kind of hope of the non-Christian, which is usually no more than a castle in the air that vanishes in a stiff wind. Grace keeps the mind from **irreversible** despair, from **permanent** hopelessness. The moment comes when a divine outlook returns. The sure movement of the second-hand of time once again sweeps with hope over the gruelling, slow moving hour-hand of darkness. Increasing despair abruptly ceases with a cry of immeasurable relief. Right in the middle of verse twenty-one we are permitted a glimpse of a holy moment. The eclipse has ended. Hope is deferred no longer. Just when the divine perspective seems forever lost a great vision of God washes over the sufferer. God has broken His silence. The servant cries, *"You have heard me. I will declare your name. I will praise you. He has not despised or disdained the suffering or the afflicted one. He has not hidden his face from him but has listened to his cry for help,"* (Psalm 22:21b-24, NIV, KJV shortened rendition). Hope has returned, and the rest of the Psalm is filled with joyous praise to God.

Who can fathom why in the purposes of God Christians must at times endure an eclipse of hope. We may never know the answer this side of heaven. Yet I suspect that this will ultimately be credited to God's glory. For in the process, there is an incongruity between what might be expected and what actually results. What might be expected, if we were limited to human resources, is a falling away; but what occurs, because of God's provision, is a willingness to trust anyway, to wait out the eclipse.

Be of good cheer, then, as Jesus said. New realities await us. God comes down to move us into places of well-being. To the non-Christians, this must seem like the worst sort of delusion. But those whom God has declared righteous carry a secret, and their lives are ruled and judged by that fact.

> *"May our Lord Jesus Christ himself and God our Father, who loved us and by his grace gave us eternal encouragement and good hope, encourage your hearts and strengthen you in every good deed and word."*
>
> (2 Thessalonians 2:16)

> *"God raised us up with Christ and seated us with him in the heavenly realms in Christ Jesus, in order that in the coming ages he might show the incomparable riches of his grace, expressed in his kindness to us in Christ Jesus."*
>
> (Ephesians 2:6-7)

The Grace Of God

These booklets are being produced as a simple introduction to basic Christian truths. Each is written in a way that can be easily understood even by 'non-readers' or those who know English as their second language. The following subjects will, in due course, be included in this developing series.

The Anointing of God
Binding and Loosing
The Blood of Christ
God's Call On Your Life
The Christian Faith
The Church
Covenants
The Cross
What Happens After Death
Deception
The Deeper Life
Deliverance
Evangelism
Faith
Fasting

Forgiveness
The Grace of God
Guidance
Hearing from God
Holiness
Holy Communion
Honour and Respect
Hope
Intercession
Prayer
Prophecy
Prosperity
Rejection
Repentance
The Resurrection
Righteousness

Servanthood
Being Slain in the Spirit
Speaking in Tongues
Spiritual Protection
Spiritual Warfare
Spirit Baptism
The State of the Lost
Temptation and How to Handle It
Tithes & Offerings
The Trinity
Trust
Water Baptism
God's Will for Your Life
Wisdom
World Mission

Prior to his conversion **CHARLES STROHMER** was deeply involved in the New Age Movement and now lectures internationally concerning its dangers. He is also a professional writer. He lives in the USA.

ISBN 1-85240-117-6

9 781852 401177

 A Sovereign World International Booklet